LIVING WITH
PURPOSE
in a WORN-OUT BODY

LIVING WITH
PURPOSE
in a WORN-OUT BODY

SPIRITUAL ENCOURAGEMENT *for* OLDER ADULTS

MISSY BUCHANAN

UPPER
ROOM BOOKS®

The Upper Room® Web site: www.upperroom.org.

UPPER ROOM®, UPPER ROOM BOOKS®, and design logos are trademarks owned by The Upper Room®, a Ministry of GBOD®, Nashville, Tennessee. All rights reserved.

Cover design: John Hamilton Design
Fourth printing: 2010

Library of Congress Cataloging-in-Publication Data

Buchanan, Missy.

  Living with purpose in a worn-out body: devotionals for frail, elderly, and those who care for them / Missy Buchanan.

     p. cm.

  ISBN 978-0-8358-9942-0

1. Older people—Prayers and devotions. I. Title.

  BV4580.B79 2008

  242'.65—dc22   2008010954

Printed in the United States of America

To the residents
of Montclair Estates Senior Residence
who invited me to share in the unvarnished truth
of their daily struggles and joys,
including Ruby Zackmire, Mary Moyer,
Rita Shoemake, Wanda and Clifford Moon, Flo
Danda, Jewell Faulkner, Elizabeth Garrett,
Barbara Gallop, Norman Duren.

To my sweet Aunt Mary
who faced each day of her ninety-five years
with an amazingly gracious spirit.

And most especially to parents,
J. J. (Mack) and Minelle McGlothlin,
who first pointed me to Christ
and modeled lives of great faith
and persistent hope.

CONTENTS

Acknowledgments

I want to acknowledge the vision of the Upper Room Books publishing staff in recognizing a great need for spiritual encouragement of the frail elderly. I also would like to recognize a special group of people whose influence on my life and faith has been profound. Thanks to my Angel Friends for being unfailing encouragers along life's journey. I also have overflowing gratitude for my children and their spouses, Matthew and Rachel, Mindy and Mike, and Beth, whose compassion for their grandparents has tendered my own heart. Finally, I want to acknowledge my husband, Barry, for loving me so well for so long. I am truly blessed beyond measure.

WHAT PURPOSE, GOD?

I confess there are days when pain suffocates my
   passion for living.

There are dark nights when fear chokes out hope.

Sometimes I wonder why you have left me on
   this earth.

I have outlived so many family and friends. Why
   do I linger?

What purpose could you have for me now?

Look at my hands. Once strong and sure, they are
   unsteady and frail.

My mind, once quick and incisive, now falters
   under the weight of names and faces.

What real purpose do I serve knitting away the
   hours, surfing the channels, dozing through
   the afternoon?

Then your Spirit stirs my heart and convicts
   my soul.

You are not a wasteful God!

The length of my earthly days is a mystery to me,
   but one thing I know for sure. You have created
   me with an eternal purpose.

How can I be more like Christ today?

Whose life can I touch with kindness?

Lord, give me an extra measure of grace when I feel that I'm too old to be useful.

Help me take my limitations in stride as I search for opportunities to serve you.

My purpose has not withered away with another birthday.

It is rooted in eternity.

PSALM 33:11

The plans of the LORD stand firm forever,
the purposes of his heart through
all generations.

EPHESIANS 1:11

In [Christ] we were also chosen, having been predestined according to the plan of him who works out everything in conformity with the purpose of his will.

SLOW MOTION

Mine is a slow-motion world where everything
　　moves like thick corn syrup.
It's a deliberate pace that is both slow and slower.
Residents with walkers inch their way to lunch.
Folks speak in measured stride.
Others lean close to hear every word.
The world says, "Hurry up. Do it faster. Faster!"
But here at the center, life crawls in turtle time.
I calculate each daily task in my mind.
How long will it take to get from here to there?
Ten minutes to the dining room some fifty
　　yards away.
A little longer to the laundry room. Longer still if
　　I'm pushing the cart.
Even mindless tasks take more time and energy.
Brushing teeth. Fastening clothes. Cutting food.
But there are small wonders to be found in
　　unhurried life.
I get to see the first bloom on the geranium outside
　　room 107.
I take in the scent of newly mown grass.
I stop and chat with the maintenance man,
　　basking in his latest fishing tale.

O God, no matter how slowly life unfolds, your
    hand is moving in the circumstances of my day.
Thanks be to you, I am moving forward still.
Glory be!

PSALM 31:14-15

I trust in you, O LORD;
    I say, "You are my God."
My times are in your hands.

2 PETER 3:13

In keeping with [God's] promise we are
looking forward to a new heaven and a new
earth, the home of righteousness.

WORRYWART

Now and then I am a real worrywart.
I fret about bladder control and outliving
    my money.
I worry about flu shots, the Middle East, and
    why the waitstaff gave me apple pie instead
    of cherry.
At times I've made myself miserable worrying
    about things out of my control.
God, why is it so hard for me to cast my burdens
    upon you?
Scripture tells me to give you my worries, but I keep
    taking them back as if I can't trust you.
Who am I to doubt the Creator's ability to deal
    with my doubts and fears?
When I am prone to worry, Lord, help me to be
    more trusting.
Show me how to release each worry in heavenward
    prayer, one by one.
In the big problems of the world and in the small
    details of my life, you are there.
You who spun the galaxies into space, now hold
    my worrywart heart.

Psalm 25:1-2

To you, O Lord, I lift up my soul;
 in you I trust, O my God.

1 Peter 5:7

Cast all your anxiety on [God] because he
cares for you.

GRANDDAUGHTER

Not so long ago I carried her in my arms and read
    her favorite good-night story to her.

I held her small hand as ocean waves lapped our
    bare feet, making us giggle with
    unbelievable joy.

But now she steadies my stooped body as I move
    from bed to chair.

It's so humbling to accept help, especially from a
    granddaughter who once thought I would
    always be able to chase after fireflies on a
    summer night.

God, where are you when the generational tables
    are turned, when the young care for the old?

Is it your plan that we learn to serve each other
    and accept being served?

Give me grace to surrender my pride, to delight in
    my granddaughter's compassion.

Let me teach her the truth about faithfulness in the
    trenches of life.

In this curious season where old and young
    intersect, may we look in each other's eyes and
    see the eyes of Christ peering back.

PSALM 25:9

[God] guides the humble in what is right
and teaches them his way.

EPHESIANS 6:7-8 (NRSV)

Render service with enthusiasm, as to the
Lord and not to men and women, knowing
that whatever good we do, we will receive the
same again from the Lord, whether we are
slaves or free.

No holding back

I have brand-new clothes I'm saving for a
    rainy day.
In fact, I've been saving them for years.
Underwear and pajamas still sealed in
    plastic wrap.
Shirts with price tags hanging from the sleeves.
Some were gifts; others were bargains. All are
    waiting for a special-enough kind of day.
O Lord, why do I act this way?
Perhaps it is how I was raised.
To work hard and save.
Certainly you want us to be good stewards, but
    now I wonder.
Have I also held back my praise to you as if I might
    one day run out?
Have I cautiously doled it out in small portions?
Where did I get the idea that worship must always
    be restrained, quiet, and dignified?
Throughout my long life, you have showered me
    with blessing upon blessing.
Today I will not withhold the praise you deserve.
Awaken the passion that I've kept tucked away for
    a rainy day.
It's all about you, Lord. Not me—but you.

Before I get out of this chair, I will lift my hands
and say aloud the Lord's Prayer. Today I will
consider what all those words mean.

I will sing a hymn of praise while I comb my hair
and put on my socks.

I will not wait for another day.

I will make a joyful noise!

PSALM 34:1-3

I will extol the LORD at all times;
 his praise will always be on my lips.
My soul will boast in the LORD;
 let the afflicted hear and rejoice.
Glorify the Lord with me;
 let us exalt his name together.

HEBREWS 12:28

Therefore, since we are receiving a kingdom
that cannot be shaken, let us be thankful,
and so worship God acceptably with
reverence and awe.

Mail

*E*ach day I look forward to the familiar sound.

Keys clinking against metal boxes, announcing that the mail has arrived.

Perhaps there will be a colorful card or a crayon drawing for my wall.

Most likely though, there will only be slick-paper ads and coupons I will never use.

No-name mail addressed to "Occupant."

Still I am anxious to peek inside the mailbox.

And even if nothing is there, you have not forgotten me.

You have sent me love letters of scripture to read again and again.

They are words of wisdom, words of encouragement and hope.

So if there is only junk mail in my box today, I will rest in the promise that my name is written on your heart.

Lord, I want to live my life as more than an "Occupant."

I want to live so that others might see who you are.

When my life seems insignificant, remind me that I still have value.

Today I will send a postcard to a neighbor who has been ill.

I will write a note to a friend just to say "I'm thinking of you."

For the price of a stamp, a fellow sojourner will be lifted up.

Postmarked: Glorious blessing.

Psalm 115:12

The Lord remembers us and will bless us.

Romans 8:17

Now if we are children, then we are heirs—heirs of God and co-heirs with Christ, if indeed we share in his sufferings in order that we may also share in his glory.

Power chair

I have learned to drive for the second time in
    my life.
This time seemed more difficult than the first.
There's no steering wheel or brake, only a
    thumbsized knob.
Who would have thought I could use two fingers
    to move around the room in
    a battery-operated chair?
I am thankful for such amazing technology.
I can maneuver the byways of the center while
    seated in a cushy chair with wheels that turn on
    a dime.
Debilitating arthritis left me too feeble to walk, and
    surgery is too risky at my age.
But I found the idea of learning to drive a
    chair unsettling.
I thought I was too old to learn anything new, but I
    was wrong.
I had to practice turning and parking again
    and again.
Lord, I confess that I have left scars and scratches
    on more than a few walls and door frames.
And along the way, I've discovered that a power
    chair is much like life.

Often I have misjudged a situation and found
　　myself smack-dab against a wall.
In those times, you have taught me to persevere.
And I have learned that without a charged battery,
　　the chair has no power.
O that I might plug my weary soul into the power
　　of your Spirit, the source of all life and goodness!

PSALM 68:35

You are awesome, O God, in your sanctuary;
　　the God of Israel gives power and strength
　　　　to his people.
Praise be to God!

ACTS 1:8

"You will receive power when the Holy Spirit
comes on you; and you will be my witnesses
in Jerusalem, and in all Judea and Samaria,
and to the ends of the earth."

LATE-IN-LIFE FRIENDS

These are not the friends who swapped campfire
  stories and ate s'mores with me.
They are not the ones whose kids played hide-and-
  seek with mine on black-velvet nights.
In fact, you won't discover them until the last few
  chapters of my life story.
They are late-in-life friends whose paths have
  crisscrossed with mine here at the senior center.
They have their own stories, their own souvenirs,
  their own friends from the past.
But all of us need late-in-life friends to come
  alongside as we complete the journey.
O Lord, keep me from staying holed up in my
  room, using it as a self-imposed prison.
Don't let me shut the door on new relationships.
Nudge me to come out and be a late-in-life friend!

PSALM 10:16-17

The LORD is King for ever and ever;
The nations will perish from his land.
You hear, O LORD, the desire of the afflicted;
    you encourage them, and you
        listen to their cry.

ROMANS 1:11-12

I long to see you so that I may impart to you
some spiritual gift to make you strong—that
is, that you and I may be mutually
encouraged by each other's faith.

I CAN'T DO IT NOW

I gave up the keys to the car. I knew it was time.
In fact, it was a relief.
But it was hard for this do-it-yourselfer to admit I
cannot do things I once could.
O Lord, my sense of independence has taken
a beating.
There are so many things I'd like to do but can't.
If I could, I would change an overhead lightbulb
and balance my checkbook.
But these tasks are hard for me now.
At times I feel humiliated by my dependence
on others.
I don't want to be a burden.
Lord, give me a humble spirit to accept
help graciously.
In my weakness you are strong.
In the mystery that is life, help me to depend on
you and trust your perfect plan.

PSALM 57:2

I cry out to God Most High,
    to God, who fulfills his purpose for me.

2 CORINTHIANS 13:4

For to be sure, he was crucified in weakness, yet he lives by God's power. Likewise, we are weak in him, yet by God's power we will live with him to serve you.

PITY PARTY

*T*ear up the invitation. The party has
    been canceled.

There will be no pity party today, though I confess I
    hurt from head to toe.

Occasionally I ache so much, I throw myself a little
    pity party. But not today.

Too much empathy can be a dangerous thing.

When I hunger for others to notice my pain, the
    party has begun.

O God, keep me from chronically feeling sorry
    for myself.

I don't want to be a drain on another's deep well
    of compassion.

Help me to accept my afflictions, knowing a better
    day is coming.

Turn my self-pity into a small act of service for
    a neighbor.

Let my hug be someone's comfort.

Let my gentle words lift another's spirit.

I will count my endless blessings, one by one, until
    pity melts into gratitude.

In all that I do, use my life to give others a glimpse
    of your eternal celebration.

This, I know, is my purpose! Alleluia!

PSALM 47:1-2

Clap your hands, all you nations;
  Shout to God with cries of joy.
How awesome is the LORD Most High,
  the great King over all the earth!

EPHESIANS 4:22-24

You were taught, with regard to your former way of life, to put off your old self, which is being corrupted by its deceitful desires; to be made new in the attitude of your minds; and to put on the new self, created to be like God in true righteousness and holiness.

CLUTTER

Some call it clutter.

I call it life.

Countless things collected over the years, making it
hard to squeeze into a small senior apartment.

How do I decide what to keep, what to sell, and
what to give away?

Some things are little snippets of life, claiming a
special place in my heart.

Faded greeting cards and my mother's
hobnail vase.

Seashells from the Caribbean and my son's first
report card.

Other things are just scattered here and there,
stockpiled in drawers and cabinets.

Lord, I don't need all the stuff I once thought I had
to have, but it's not easy to let it go.

Keep me from being burdened down with piles and
stacks of who knows what.

Help me sort through the clutter and remember
that things of this world are only temporary.

Show me how to lighten my load, knowing that my
eternal inheritance awaits.

Psalm 119:37

Turn my eyes away from worthless things;
  preserve my life according to your word.

Matthew 6:19-20

"Do not store up for yourselves treasures on earth, where moth and rust destroy, and where thieves break in and steal. But store up for yourselves treasures in heaven, where moth and rust do not destroy, and where thieves do not break in and steal."

LIFE AND DEATH

There are daily announcements in the
dining room.

You can read them on bulletin boards and
oversized calendars too.

In the midst of news about a grocery store outing
and afternoon dominoes, there's an update on a
resident who's now in ICU.

At a senior center, ambulances come and go,
stirring questions about who and what.

Here one cannot deny death. It cannot be glossed
over or ignored.

It is a part of everyday life, and sometimes the
announcements serve as sobering reminders of
our mortality.

Here at the center, life and death ebb and flow in a
strangely natural way.

But because of the Cross, I live with reassurance
that my future is secure. Eternity is mine.

I rejoice in the promise!

Psalm 89:48 (NRSV)

Who can live and never see death?
Who can escape the power of Sheol?

Romans 6:23

For the wages of sin is death, but the gift of God is eternal life in Christ Jesus our Lord.

GOOD NIGHT'S SLEEP

It's been a long day, a very long day.

I feel used up and wrung out.

I struggle to turn back the covers on my bed.

Even changing into my nightclothes has been quite
an ordeal.

On nights like this I want to shake my fist and cry
out to you, "Why is growing old so hard?"

The sun has barely dipped behind the horizon and
already I long for a night of good rest.

Wrap me in your calming presence, Lord.

Refresh my body and mind with hours and hours
of uninterrupted sleep.

As my eyes close tonight, let my mind come to rest
in you.

Sweet, sweet sleep.

PSALM 116:7

Be at rest once more, O my soul,
    for the LORD has been good to you.

MATTHEW 11:28-29

"Come to me, all you who are weary and
burdened, and I will give you rest. . . . For I
am gentle and humble in heart, and you will
find rest for your souls."

Around the Table

Above the muffled conversation, there is a gentle
    clattering of rolling carts and ice in glasses.

It's lunchtime, and I am grateful for this time of
    fellowship and food.

Once strangers, now friends, we sit around the
    table, bringing different tastes acquired over
    decades of life experiences.

Too much pepper. Not enough. Too sweet. Too sour.
    Just right.

Around the table, we are community, where
    relationships are more important than food.

It is here that we exchange bragging rights about a
    granddaughter's new job or a nephew's award.

Here we share laughter and stories, aches
    and pains.

Some of us wear oversized bibs around our necks, a
    practical solution to spills and such.

We are Baptists and Methodists, Catholics and
    evangelicals, and some who have rarely
    darkened a church door.

But around the table, no one is impressed by
    denominational platitude. We are simply
    sojourners together.

The table is a place of connectedness where
    someone notices and cares if you are not there.

O God, you have made us a people who
    crave relationship.
You have made us hungry for love and respect, no
    matter our age.
And you have given us a holy appetite for you.
Fill us up, Lord!

PSALM 34:8 (NRSV)

O taste and see that the LORD is good;
    happy are those who take refuge in him.

HEBREWS 10:25

Let us not give up meeting together, as
some are in the habit of doing, but let us
encourage one another—and all the more
as you see the Day approaching.

ORDINARY DAYS

There's a slow, steady rhythm to ordinary days.

Uneventful kind of days that follow a simple
routine of meals, medications, and favorite
TV shows.

During this time, empty squares march across
the calendar.

One day feels like the next.

In truth, I like days that are uninterrupted by crisis
or sudden change.

I am thankful for the repetition.

But Lord, it's easy to get lost in the monotony.

Save me from the emptiness that comes with too
much time to think and too little to do. It is
fertile soil for negative thoughts to grow.

And if I hold too tightly to rigid routine, remind me
that I may miss out on a wonderful surprise.

Help me rediscover the abundant blessings in
my life.

Today I will turn the pages of an old photo album,
and I will give you thanks for my life stories.

I will pray for my loved ones, calling each
by name.

O Lord, show me the extraordinary joy in
ordinary days.

PSALM 19:8

The precepts of the LORD are right,
  giving joy to the heart.
The commands of the LORD are radiant,
  giving light to the eyes.

ROMANS 12:11-13

Never be lacking in zeal, but keep your
spiritual fervor, serving the Lord. Be joyful in
hope, patient in affliction, faithful in prayer.
Share with God's people who are in need.
Practice hospitality.

MEDICINE BOTTLES

Plastic brown cylinders line the shelf.

Prescription medications with hard-to-pronounce
names and countless possible side effects.

Medications provide a better quality of life; at least
that's what the commercials say.

Twice daily. Once in the morning. Take with food.
One at bedtime.

For blood pressure and high cholesterol, for
arthritis and sleeping aid.

It seems so strange that my world revolves around
pills and capsules.

More than the greatest miracles of modern
medicine is the miracle of your love. You have
placed immeasurable value on my life—not
because I deserve it but because of who you are.

O Lord, you are the great Physician whose will for
my life is wellness and restoration.

Give me a daily dose of humor that eases the pain.

Supply me with the balm of encouragement that
overcomes fatigue.

Let me respond in prayer and praise.

Above all, help me to keep my eyes on you, the
Healer of broken lives and timeworn bodies.

PSALM 6:2

Be merciful to me, LORD, for I am faint;
O LORD, heal me, for my bones are in agony.

MATTHEW 4:23

Jesus went throughout Galilee, teaching in their synagogues, preaching the good news of the kingdom, and healing every disease and sickness among the people.

Sin

I'd like to believe there's a moment in time when
I've outlived the ability to sin.

I'd like to believe it, but I can't because it's not true.

Even at my ripe age, I am a sinner.

Forgive me when I am stiff-necked and rebellious,
more passionate about how-life-used-to-be than
about you.

Forgive me when I give a judgmental stare at a
neighbor who's different from me.

Lord, I know there are days when I am cranky and
complain about insignificant things.

Convict my spirit. Forgive me, your elderly child.

Please hear this earnest prayer of confession.

Cover me in your grace, and help me daily to grow
up as I grow older still.

PSALM 51:1-4

Have mercy on me, O God,
    according to your unfailing love;
according to your great compassion
    blot out my transgressions.
Wash away all my iniquity
    and cleanse me from my sin.
For I know my transgressions,
    and my sin is always before me.
Against you, you only, have I sinned
    and done what is evil in your sight,
so that you are proved right when you
    speak and justified when you judge.

MATTHEW 6:14 (NRSV)

"For if you forgive others their trespasses,
your heavenly Father will also forgive you."

BINGO

By midafternoon, people shuffle to the dining
    room, anxious to play away an hour or two.
It's time for bingo at the center.
Large, bold-lettered cards are spread across
    the tables.
Some folks fiddle with hearing aids and eyeglasses
    as the numbers are announced aloud. B-12.
    G-52. I-27.
Finally a voice calls out in excitement like a child
    who knows the answer to a teacher's question.
Bingo! Bingo!
O God, can such silly tomfoolery be a part of
    your design?
Keep me from being the gray-haired stick-in-the-
    mud I never wanted to be.
Give me joy in this journey until its end.
When I am tempted to be discouraged or grumpy,
    awaken my sense of fun!
Surely in the simple pleasures of a game . . . in the
    laughter and camaraderie, there is a glimpse of
    the kingdom to come.
 Hallelujah!

Psalm 133:1 (NRSV)

How very good and pleasant it is
    when kindred live together in unity!

1 Thessalonians 5:11

Therefore encourage one another and build
each other up, just as in fact you are doing.

JUST HERE

Just here.

That's how I feel today.

I'm just here.

Stalled out.

Little more than taking up space.

It seems I'm just marking time until you are ready
to take me home, God.

Going through the motions of living without really
being alive.

Marching in the same place over and over, day
after day.

Going nowhere. Just here.

Lord, help me wrestle with this sluggish depression.

Sweep away my gloomy spirit.

Change the way I see life.

Let me find the tiny ray of sunlight that pierces the
darkest clouds.

I will glorify you one day at a time, one hour at
a time.

Blessed be the name of the Lord who lifts me up
from the abyss of Just Here.

PSALM 42:1-4 (NRSV)

As a deer longs for flowing streams,
　　so my soul longs for you, O God.
My soul thirsts for God, for the living God.
When shall I come and behold the face of God?
My tears have been my food day and night,
while people say to me continually,
　　"Where is your God?"
These things I remember,
　　as I pour out my soul:
how I went with the throng,and led them
　　in procession to the house of God,
with glad shouts and songs of thanksgiving,
　　a multitude keeping festival.

ROMANS 12:2 (NRSV)

Do not be conformed to this world, but be
transformed by the renewing of your minds,
so that you may discern what is the will of
God—what is good and acceptable
and perfect.

WHITTLED-DOWN WORLD

I have seen the many wonders of your world,
　　O God.

Not so long ago, I picked wildflowers in green
　　meadows and hopscotched through
　　mountain streams.

I wiggled my toes in sugar-white sand and lifted
　　my face to the saltwater spray.

Your creation is so vast; the universe so grand.

But now, my world is whittled down to a
　　comfortable apartment in a senior complex
　　where walkers and power chairs navigate the
　　sidewalks like gondolas on the Grand Canal.

My days are anchored to an easy chair, with only
　　trips to the doctor and special occasions to take
　　me beyond this place that is home.

Though I am limited by space and physical
　　mobility, my God is not.

Daily I am reminded that this is my Father's world.

Around the corner I catch the fragrance of a rose,
　　drifting on a warm breeze.

From my porch I watch a crimson maple leaf
　　flutter against an autumn sky.

I celebrate the pattern of shadow and light created
　　by the sun shining through porch railings.

These simple things point me to you, O God,
   Creator of all.
 Bless this whittled-down world and all who dwell
   in it.

PSALM 50:12

For the world is mine, and all that is in it.

ROMANS 1:20 (NRSV)

Ever since the creation of the world [God's]
eternal power and divine nature, invisible
though they are, have been understood and
seen through the things he has made. So they
are without excuse.

Forgotten

Is it possible to be loved and forgotten at the
   same time?

Sometimes that's how I feel.

Loved but forgotten, like a once-cherished doll left
   on a top shelf.

Outside my senior center, friends and family buzz
   from place to place.

They have good intentions, but their lives are
   crowded with jobs and soccer games, church
   events and fast food.

It seems I am the last thing on their long to-do lists.

O God, you hear the cry of my mixed-up heart,
   and you love me still.

When I feel abandoned by others, let me rejoice in
   knowing that you will never forget one of
   your own.

You will never leave me like a doll on a shelf.

If I want friends and family to remember me, let
   me remember them.

I will phone a loved one and listen attentively to
   the ups and downs of her day.

I will chase away loneliness by knocking on the
   door of a neighbor, sharing a cookie or two.

Lord, help me press on, keeping my eye on you.

I am not forgotten. I am redeemed!

Psalm 16:9-10

Therefore my heart is glad and
    my tongue rejoices;
    my body also will rest secure,
because you will not abandon me
    to the grave,
    nor will you let your Holy One see decay.

Luke 12:6-7

"Are not five sparrows sold for two pennies?
Yet not one of them is forgotten by God.
Indeed, the very hairs of your head are all
numbered. Don't be afraid; you are worth
more than many sparrows."

LAUGHTER

There's laughter at the center.

With little prompting, smiles spread easily across wrinkled faces.

On Tuesday morning tap dancers in feather boas entertain in lively style.

On Friday afternoon there's an Elvis impersonator in blue-suede shoes.

In the dining room there are silly jokes that I forget even before dessert is served.

O Lord, I feel your presence in the sweet fragrance of laughter.

Gentle laughter that makes old eyes sparkle again.

When I am down, its infectious sound lifts me up.

Thank you for laughter that smooths the sharp rocks of life.

Today I will laugh with unrestrained joy!

Joyful, joyful, we adore thee!

PSALM 126:1-2 (NRSV)

When the LORD restored the fortunes of Zion,
    we were like those who dream.
Then our mouth was filled with laughter,
    and our tongue with shouts of joy;
      then it was said among the nations,
"The LORD has done great things for them."

LUKE 6:20-21

Looking at his disciples, [Jesus] said:
"Blessed are you who are poor,
    for yours is the kingdom of God.
Blessed are you who hunger now,
    for you will be satisfied.
Blessed are you who weep now,
    for you will laugh."

LIFELINE

There's a telephone at my fingertips.

It's my connection to friends and family miles away or just a few doors down. It's a way to chat away the isolation.

On the wall there's a button I can push if there's an emergency.

I wear another button around my neck to alert someone if I fall or start to feel faint.

Each is a lifeline linking me to another.

And so it is with prayer.

It is my lifeline to you, O God.

But why do I wait until there's a crisis, frantically pushing the button of prayer. Help me! Help me, now, Lord!

Father, show me how to have an ongoing conversation with you.

Easy conversation about all the things on my heart.

I will pray my way through this day, knowing that you hear every word.

O the wonder of a lifeline.

PSALM 17:6

I call on you, O God, for you will answer me;
give ear to me and hear my prayer.

1 THESSALONIANS 5:16-18

Be joyful always; pray continually; give
thanks in all circumstances, for this is God's
will for you in Christ Jesus.

Loss

You would think after so many years, it might be
  easier to accept loss. But it's not.

Bidding an earthly farewell is hard, Lord, even at
  my age.

We had often talked about who would go first, who
  might better carry on without the other, as if it
  were in our control.

But of course, it's not.

It hurts to reach for the hand that is not there.

I especially miss the conversation at night, the
  pillow talk about a grandson's dream and
  today's fried chicken.

These sunset years are bittersweet.

Silence can be a lonely sound.

Tears gather when I think of all the life stories we
  created together.

In the solitude of the afternoon, I sometimes sink
  into sadness.

Shore up my sagging spirit, God.

There is comfort in knowing that even Jesus wept.

You never said the journey would be without pain
  or struggle.

But you have promised that eternity will be worth
  every step.

One day I will celebrate with loved ones who wait
for me there.
I believe. O yes, I believe!

PSALM 34:18

The LORD is close to the brokenhearted
and saves those who are crushed in spirit.

JOHN 16:20

"You will grieve, but your grief will turn
to joy."

HOPE

Lord, I need a big dose of hope today.

None of the pie-in-the-sky kind.

Not even a pretty-sure guess.

I need the real kind of hope that brings lightness to a heavy day.

I am tired of gritting my teeth, trying to swallow the pain that is my reality.

When I look back on my life, I see how you proved faithful time after time.

There were moments I thought you had forgotten me only to discover you were holding me so close I couldn't see.

So if the stubborn pain refuses to subside for a while, I will still whisper your name in praise.

Refocus my mind on you, Lord. Only on you.

It is there I find hope.

Psalm 31:24

Be strong and take heart,
  all you who hope in the Lord.

Romans 15:4

For everything that was written in the past was written to teach us, so that through endurance and the encouragement of the Scriptures we might have hope.

GIFT OF LONG LIFE

Sometimes I wonder if long life is really a gift.
Bone-tired and weak, I can't even open a jar
   of jelly.
I feel so useless.
Then I begin to think of the many blessings long
   life has provided.
I have watched children and grandchildren grow
   from chubby-cheeked toddlers to
   remarkable adults.
Tears of joy have filled my eyes at countless
   graduations and weddings.
My life has been chockful of Christmas mornings
   and summer vacations.
These are the special gifts of long life.
Tender memories that make me rich
   beyond measure.
It's true I have known heights and depths, both joy
   and heartache.
But through it all, you have been faithful.
May the footprints I leave behind my long life
   guide others to you.
I accept today as yet another gift.
I will open it with a grateful heart knowing I have
   purpose in this day.
To thine be the glory!

Psalm 92:14-15

They will still bear fruit in old age,
    they will stay fresh and green,
proclaiming, "The Lord is upright;
    he is my Rock, and there is no
    wickedness in him."

Philippians 1:4-6

In all my prayers for all of you, I always pray with joy because of your partnership in the gospel from the first day until now, being confident of this, that he who began a good work in you will carry it on to completion until the day of Christ Jesus.

TONGUE

O Lord, sometimes I say things before I think.

In my frustration, words tumble out, and I wish I
could take them back.

Today I cry out in private prayer.

Help me control my tongue.

Old age gives no license for prejudice or self-
righteous pride.

Forgive me when I am puffed up in arrogance,
thinking I've earned the right to be sharp
and severe.

When my words are harsh or hurtful, convict my
critical spirit.

Replace gossip or sarcasm with words that soothe
and build up.

Put kindness on my lips and sensitivity in my heart
for every neighbor, caregiver, employee, and
family member.

I want to be a pleasure to be around, even if others
are not.

Let my tongue be an instrument to bring you glory.

PSALM 37:30 (NRSV)

The mouths of the righteous utter wisdom,
   and their tongues speak justice.

JAMES 3:9-10 (NRSV)

With [the tongue] we bless the Lord and
Father, and with it we curse those who are
made in the likeness of God. From the same
mouth come blessing and cursing. My
brothers and sisters, this ought not to be so.

BEGINNING A NEW DAY

The sun announces a new day, and already I'm
filled with dread.

After a restless night, the morning seems more a
burden than a blessing.

O God, where is the joy when dawn brings another
struggle just to get out of bed?

I am weary and frustrated by a body that fails me.

How I long to see and hear without aid, to move
without aching, to dance in easy abandon.

O Lord, give me grace to meet every challenge that
comes today.

Give me your supernatural strength to be better
not bitter.

Turn my despair into divine delight.

Though my feet can't dance, my heart will.

Though my hands fumble, I will lift them up
in praise.

Though my mouth struggles to make sense, I will
share my smile with another.

Let me never be too old to grow in faith.

Let me be lost in the wonder of worship.

Bring on the new day!

Psalm 143:8

Let the morning bring me word
of your unfailing love,
for I have put my trust in you.
Show me the way I should go,
for to you I lift up my soul.

Philippians 2:12-13

Continue to work out your salvation with
fear and trembling, for it is God who works in
you to will and to act according to his
good purpose.

Church

God, I miss my church.

I know it is more than a building, but I miss the familiar stained-glass windows that spill colorful patterns across the sanctuary floor.

I miss the organ music that fills sacred space.

I long to touch the pew with a peculiar knothole in the wood grain.

Decades of worship, so many memories.

Of baptisms and funerals, of weddings and potluck dinners.

I wish I could kneel at the altar once again and stretch out my hands to accept the sacrament of Communion.

I want to stand with friends and family and lift our voices together in grateful praise.

But now the journey to church has become too strenuous for my frail body.

Here at home, I fumble through the pages of my Bible and struggle to concentrate on each passage.

How I wish my bent body could walk upright into the familiar sanctuary.

But I can worship you anywhere . . . from my bed or in my chair.

I am in your presence. Praise be!

PSALM 95:6-7

Come, let us bow down in worship,
   let us kneel before the LORD our Maker;
for he is our God
   and we are the people of his pasture,
   the flock under his care.

LUKE 2:36-37

She was very old; she had lived with her husband seven years after her marriage, and then was a widow until she was eighty-four. She never left the temple but worshiped night and day, fasting and praying.

NOT THE END OF THE STORY

They say every good story must have a beginning,
   a middle, and an end.

I suppose that is true for novels and fairy tales too.

For my own life story, the beginning and middle
   were written years ago, but not the
   final chapters.

So far, it's been an interesting story with twists and
   turns in the plot.

And if I look carefully, I see evidence of your
   faithfulness written on every page.

Lord, I still don't know how the last few paragraphs
   will unfold.

I'm not sure when I will draw my final breath.

But I do know for certain, the story won't end there.

Your promise of eternal life gives real meaning to
   the fairy-tale ending: "And they lived happily
   ever after."

PSALM 119:89-90

Your word, O LORD, is eternal;
    it stands firm in the heavens.
Your faithfulness continues
    through all generations;
you established the earth, and it endures.

JOHN 3:16

"For God so loved the world that he gave his one and only Son, that whoever believes in him shall not perish but have eternal life."

THEY DO NOT UNDERSTAND

They don't understand.

I can see the uncomfortable look in the eyes of
those whose occasional visit to the senior center
is viewed as a dreaded obligation.

The sight of elderly people with worn-out bodies
makes them uneasy.

They are visitors who come at holiday time,
bearing pasted-on smiles and cheerful trinkets.

I notice they duck their heads and look away as if
old age is too painful to witness.

I can almost hear their silent pleas, "O God, don't
let me ever live like this."

They'd rather not see the realities of growing old.

But they do not understand.

This place is our Bethesda, the spring-fed pool where
invalids and outcasts gathered in Bible times.

It is Jesus who meets us here. He seeks those whose
bodies are bent. He welcomes those who spill
food in their laps.

Here he heals our broken spirits.

I want to shout to the visitors and say, "Don't look
away. I am an exquisite child of God!"

Lord, give me strength to bear their pity.

Give them hearts that are tender and hands that
serve in humility.

For one day, they too may gather, hunched and
frail, at the pool of Bethesda.

PSALM 41:1

Blessed is [the one] who has regard for
the weak;
The LORD delivers . . . in times of trouble.

JOHN 5:3-9

Here a great number of disabled people used
to lie—the blind, the lame, the paralyzed. One
who was there had been an invalid for thirty-
eight years. When Jesus saw him lying there
and learned that he had been in this condition
for a long time, he asked him, "Do you want
to get well?"

"Sir," the invalid replied, "I have no one to
help me into the pool when the water is
stirred. While I am trying to get in, someone
else goes down ahead of me."

Then Jesus said to him, "Get up! Pick up
your mat and walk." At once the man was
cured; he picked up his mat and walked.

SENSIBLE SHOES

I have several pairs of shoes on the bottom of
　　my closet.

All are sensible in an unfashionable kind of way.

They are practical with thick, nonskid soles, easy to
　　slip on and off, some with adhesive strips
　　instead of ties.

I keep my favorite pair nestled under the edge of
　　my bed within easy reach.

Sensible shoes are snug enough but not too tight,
　　just right for calloused feet with yellowing nails.

Today when I put on my sensible shoes, I will say a
　　prayer for children around the world who
　　have none.

When I stroke my swollen ankles, I will say a word
　　of thanks that I can still walk.

O Lord, give me hope beyond reason, faith beyond
　　common sense, life beyond old age.

On this day, let these sensible shoes walk close
　　to you.

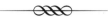

Psalm 37:23-24

Our steps are made firm by the Lord,
when he delights in our way;
though we stumble, we shall not fall
headlong,
for the Lord holds us by the hand.

James 4:8

Come near to God and he will come near
to you.

Shadow of death

How many times have I heard a minister read the
    Twenty-third Psalm at the funeral of a
    loved one?
How many times have I traced the scripture with
    my finger?

"The Lord is my shepherd,
    I shall not be in want.
He makes me lie down in green pastures,
he leads me beside quiet waters,
        he restores my soul.
He guides me in paths of righteousness
    for his name's sake.
Even though I walk through the valley of the
    shadow of death,
I will fear no evil, for you are with me; your rod
    and your staff, they comfort me."

I wonder what it really means to walk through the
    valley of the shadow of death?
When I read these words, my mind conjures up
    rocky cliffs and deep ravines.
I tremble at the thought of a journey to
    an unknown place.

But in your mercy, God, you draw me to these
familiar words once again, bringing revelation
and comfort.

To walk through. Not to stop or stay but to
pass through.

Not the valley of death but the valley of the *shadow*
of death.

If there is shadow, there must also be light.

Your Word promises me that Jesus is the light of
the world!

I will fear no evil.

Praise God for the fullness of light that will safely
lead me home.

PSALM 56:3-4 (NRSV)

When I am afraid,
    I put my trust in you.
In God, whose word I praise,
    in God I trust; I am not afraid;
    what can flesh do to me?

MATTHEW 4:16

The people living in darkness
have seen a great light;
on those living in the land of the
shadow of death
a light has dawned.

FORGIVENESS

*F*or all these years, I've kept it buried like a
  hot coal.

Burning resentment.

A business associate betrayed me decades ago.

A neighbor said unkind things about my child.

A family member left me wounded on the roadside
  of life.

And ever since, I've pushed down the hurt until I
  couldn't see it anymore.

I thought over time the coal would die out into a
  cold lump of nothingness, but it didn't.

It still glows hot in the deepest crevice of my heart.

For years I longed to hear an apology, but I never
  got it.

Most likely, I never will.

But I've let the hurt smolder far too long.

Forgiveness is not easy, even when you are old.

Lord, I cannot do this alone.

Let the cool water of your grace flow over me until
  the burning coal is finally doused.

You have forgiven me again and again.

How can I not do the same?

PSALM 130:3-4

If you, O Lord, kept a record of sins,
   O Lord, who could stand?
But with you there is forgiveness;
   therefore you are feared.

COLOSSIANS 3:13

Bear with each other and forgive whatever grievances you may have against one another. Forgive as the Lord forgave you.

Music

Nothing invigorates my soul like the sound of familiar hymns and songs of praise.

When I am feeling down, they lift my spirit as answered prayer.

Tender melodies. Timeless harmony.

Reassurance of a better tomorrow.

Some are quiet and tender; others make me tap the table in rhythm.

O Lord, though my voice is weak, my heart cannot be silent!

My mind cannot recall every lyric, but my soul cries out with unspeakable joy.

Today I will join the voices of Paul and Silas, singing midnight songs of praise.

Today I will outsing the angels!

Praise be to you, O God!

PSALM 30:4

Sing to the LORD, you saints of his;
  praise his holy name.

ACTS 16:25

About midnight Paul and Silas were praying
and singing hymns to God, and the other
prisoners were listening to them.

FEAR

Some days I am wrought with fear.

A private battle with what-ifs and what-thens.

O Lord, I admit I am terrified of ambulances and
medical tests.

Of bad news, broken bones, and drawn-out illness.

Here I am at this late date, and I'm afraid I don't
even know the Bible as I should.

I feel so vulnerable, Lord.

Lift me out of this pit of despair and draw me close.

You who stilled the waters, please still my
anxious heart.

Protect me from my deepest fears.

You alone are my refuge and strength.

Your grace supplies all that I need to endure, for I
have a divine mission to fulfill.

Psalm 27:1

The Lord is my light and my salvation—
  whom shall I fear?
The Lord is the stronghold of my life—
  of whom shall I be afraid?

Romans 8:38-39

For I am convinced that neither death nor
life, neither angels nor demons, neither the
present nor the future, nor any powers,
neither height nor depth, nor anything else
in all creation, will be able to separate us
from the love of God that is in Christ Jesus
our Lord.

BREATHING

O God, sometimes I can barely breathe.

It's hardest when it's too hot, too cold, or
 too polluted.

On those days I struggle for even a shallow breath.

Gasping for air like a scared youngster learning
 to swim.

I try to muffle the desperate sound, but I can't.

I stay inside and nervously look out the window as
 the world goes by.

O God, this is not how I wanted life to be.

Tethered to an oxygen tank by a tube in my nose.

Tired after a short walk.

Rushing to take another breathing treatment with
 inhalers and nebulizers.

What I wouldn't give for an easy breath that fills
 me up.

O Lord, I am reminded that you gave everything to
 fill me up.

You gave your Son that I might live long after my
 last breath.

HEBREWS 13:5

God has said,
  "Never will I leave you;
    never will I forsake you."

ACTS 17:24-25 (NRSV)

"The God who made the world and everything in it, he who is Lord of heaven and earth, does not live in shrines made by human hands, nor is he served by human hands, as though he needed anything, since he himself gives to all mortals life and breath and all things."

LEGACY

When I'm gone, I pray my family and friends will carry on.

Not just move on but carry on a legacy of faith.

I will leave behind a few pieces of jewelry, my father's hand-carved walking stick, and the rest of my retirement fund.

But I can't leave them a portion of faith.

There is no such thing as secondhand faith.

I think I've felt too awkward to talk about spiritual things with those I love most. I don't even know why.

O God, give me the words to say and the courage to say them.

About the miracles I've witnessed.

About how you have been faithful even when I have not.

I want them to understand it's not just about being good, moral people. It's not even about doing noble things.

It's about you. It's all about glorifying you.

In this winter of my life, let the fire of my faith shine brightly that they might see.

It's all for your glory!

PSALM 89:1

I will sing of the LORD's great love forever;
   with my mouth I will make your
faithfulness known
   through all generations

LUKE 1:50

"[God's] mercy extends to those who fear
him, from generation to generation."

HOMESICK

*H*omesick at ninety-two?

Being homesick makes sense for a seven-year-old
   child leaving for camp.

But I am very old.

Why am I so restless for home?

I believe it's because you made me that way, God.

You created me with an earthly body but a
   heavenly spirit that yearns to be with you.

This world is not my home. Not really.

I can recall every nook and cranny of the old
   home place.

It's where I raised my family and stood at the
   kitchen sink.

Those vivid memories bring comfort and joy.

But as wonderful as it was, heaven is better.

You promise it is beyond my imagination, a place
   where pain and worry do not exist.

On some days I wonder how much longer, God.

It seems I'm taking the long way home.

But it's been quite a journey.

Quite a journey indeed. And it's not over yet.

Let there be praise on my lips and worship in
   my heart!

Psalm 63:3-4

Because your love is better than life,
    my lips will glorify you.
I will praise you as long as I live,
    and in your name I will lift up my hands.

1 Corinthians 2:9

However, as it is written:
"No eye has seen,
    no ear has heard,
no mind has conceived
    what God has prepared for those who
        love him."

Doubts

When you get to be my age, you're supposed to have it all figured out, or at least that's what I used to think.

I don't think that any more.

There are moments when I believe and doubt at the same time.

I suppose some of us old folks are just too proud to admit we have doubts, especially about the hard questions of life.

Why do innocent babies die and greedy people get rich?

If you love me so much, why have you brought me to this painful season?

There were times in my life when I thought you would work a certain way, but you didn't.

A loved one was not cured. A career was never realized. A dream was not fulfilled.

Sometimes I hear people spew all the right answers about you, but they frighten me more than occasional doubts.

O Lord, give me authentic faith. Real, nitty-gritty faith for moments when I doubt.

I believe. Help me in my unbelief.

PSALM 42:11

Why are you downcast, O my soul?
  Why so disturbed within me?
Put your hope in God,
  for I will yet praise him,
  my Savior and my God.

JOHN 20:27

Then he said to Thomas, "Put your finger here; see my hands. Reach out your hand and put it into my side. Stop doubting and believe."

AGING WELL

What does it mean to age well?

Is it to be mentally sharp or to look years younger than your age?

God, I believe you intend that aging well is not about appearance or quick recall.

To age well is to bend my will to yours.

Only then can you use every situation to make me more like Jesus.

Lord, I am old, but I want to be a vessel of humility and grace that can be poured out onto the lives of others.

That, I believe, is the secret of aging well.

PSALM 40:8

"I desire to do your will, O my God;
    your law is within my heart."

COLOSSIANS 3:12

Therefore, as God's chosen people, holy and dearly loved, clothe yourselves with compassion, kindness, humility, gentleness and patience.

About the Author

———∞∞∞———

MISSY BUCHANAN, a native Texan and former educator, lives in Rockwall, Texas, with her husband, Barry. She is the cofounder of Something to Celebrate, a business dedicated to helping women utilize their God-given creative gifts. She writes a regular monthly column, "Aging Well," for *The United Methodist Reporter*.

The writing of this book is Missy's response to her spiritual calling as a daughter and caregiver to her parents in the most tender season of their lives. Her father died in March of 2006. Her ninety-two-year-old mother (May 2008) continues to seek purpose in her life, but increasing pain and health issues add to her difficulty.

Visit Missy's Web site to learn more:

www.missybuchanan.com